Saskatchewan Handmade and Home-Based Listings 2019

4 Paws Games and Publishing

Bruno, Saskatchewan, Canada

Saskatchewan Handmade and Home-Based Listings 2019

Compiled and written by 4 Paws Games and Publishing

Cover Art by 4 Paws Games and Publishing

Edited by 4 Paws Games and Publishing

Formatted and Published by 4 Paws Games and Publishing

First publication

Published January 2019

ISBN-13: 978-1-988345-94-9

Published by 4 Paws Games and Publishing

P.O. Box 444

Humboldt, Saskatchewan, Canada S0K 2A0

http://www.4-Paws-Games-and-Publishing.ca

TABLE OF CONTENTS

BIGGAR

Direct Sellers

Business Name: Henrietta Parenteau – Independent Voxxlife Associate

Name: Henrietta Parenteau

Address: Box 635 Biggar, SK S0K 0M0

Email: henrietta.parenteau@sasktel.net

Website: www.voxxlife.com/henrietta

Social Media: www.facebook.com/groups/1783904981726572

Products Sold: Wellness boot, non-slip, and athletic socks. Athletic socks come in no show, mini crew, and knee-high insoles and patches.

Tradeshows

Event Name: Red, White and Gold Tradeshow

Date and Time: June 30, 2019 10AM-4PM

Event Address: ½ mile North of Biggar on Highway 4

Organizer Name: Biggar Rec Valley; Henrietta Parenteau

Organizer Phone: 306-948-6413

Description: Open to all types of vendors.

Vendor Types Accepted: Mixed variety.

BRUNO

Business Name: 4 Paws Games and Publishing

Name: Vickianne Caswell

Address: Box 444 Humboldt, SK S0K 2A0

Phone: 639-994-7297 or 639-994-PAWS

Email: Admin@4-Paws-Games-and-Publishing.ca

Website: www.4-Paws-Games-and-Publishing.ca

Social Media: www.facebook.com/4.Paws.Games.and.Publishing

Products Sold: Books, e-books, and series merchandise.

Service: Mystery parties, event planning, author services, event planning, social media, and some website services, ECWID® store setup, photo videos, SK event advertising, image, and file conversions, and more.

Business Name: The Garage Gallery

Name: Robin Renneberg

Address: 530 Main Street

Email: beyondthemomentdesigns@gmail.com

Website: www.thegaragegallerybruno.com

Social Media: www.facebook.com/thegaragegallerybruno

Products Sold: Saskatchewan artwork including, but not limited to acrylic paintings, sculptures, wood turning, handcrafted jewellery and wooden boxes.

Event Name: Bruno Easter Eggstravaganza

Date and Time: April 6, 2019. 10AM-4PM

Event Address: 513 Kirby Street, Bruno Community Hall

Website: https://www.4-paws-games-and-publishing.ca/brunoeastereggstravaganza2019.html

Social Media: https://www.facebook.com/BrunoEasterEggtravaganza

Event Description: Come and enjoy some shopping at the second annual "Easter Eggstravaganza." Home-based business products, baking, crafts, books and more. A colouring table courtesy of Freckles the Bunny Series, items for kids to buy, paint and then take home. Kids tattoos, and free coffee. Come visit Poohka the rabbit between 11AM-2PM. The first 50 kids will get a treat (Poohka and the treat are free). Spots are $30 for a table and 2 chairs or 2 tables/$50.

Free admission. Kitchen is being run a local group fundraising and the door prizes will support the Bruno Friendship Centre which occurred water damage this year. Should this change, we will announce the change on our Facebook page and announce another group to help.

Organizer Name: 4 Paws Games and Publishing; Vickianne Caswell

Organizer Phone: 639-994-7297 or 639-994-PAWS

Organizer Email: Admin@4-Paws-Games-and-Publishing.ca

Vendor Types Accepted: Mixed variety.

Event Name: The Creative Expressions Experience

Date and Time: September 28, 2019, 10AM-4PM

Event Address: 513 Kirby Street, Bruno Community Hall

Website: www.4-paws-games-and-publishing.ca/creativeexpressionsevent2019.html

Social Media: www.facebook.com/CreativeExpressionsExperience

Event Description: Join us for our third annual Creative Expressions event held in Bruno, Saskatchewan. The event is a way to share what artistic talents people have through crafts, their voices, dance, writing and more. Holding entertainment such as readings from some great authors, vocalists, crafts and so much more. A family-friendly event that has some activities for the children, and a variety of hand-crafted

Come volunteer as entertainment or help for the day, vend with us, or simply come out and see what it's about! Vendors, sponsors, volunteers, and demonstrators wanted! Hosted by 4 Paws Games and Publishing.

Organizer Name: 4 Paws Games and Publishing; Vickianne Caswell

Organizer Phone: 639-994-7297 or 639-994-PAWS

Organizer Email: Admin@4-Paws-Games-and-Publishing.ca

Vendor Types Accepted: Handmade, artistic, cosplay and select products only.

Event Name: Bruno Stocking Stuffer

Date and Time: November 30, 2019, 10AM-4PM

Event Address: 513 Kirby Street, Bruno Community Hall

Website: https://www.4-paws-games-and-publishing.ca/brunostockingstuffer2019.html

Social Media: https://www.facebook.com/BrunoStockingStuffer

Event Description: Bruno's annual "Stocking Stuffer" event, brings in 200+ shoppers. Home-based business products, baking, crafts, books and more. A colouring table courtesy of Freckles the Bunny Series, items for kids to buy, paint and then take home. Kids tattoos, a "Cutest Christmas Kid" contest, free coffee, and door prizes. Come visit Santa between 11AM-2PM. The first 50 kids will get a treat (Santa and the treat are free). Spots are $30 for a table and 2 chairs or 2 tables/$50. Free admission.

Organizer Name: 4 Paws Games and Publishing; Vickianne Caswell

Organizer Phone: 639-994-7297 or 639-994-PAWS

Organizer Email: Admin@4-Paws-Games-and-Publishing.ca

Vendor Types Accepted: Mixed variety.

CRAVEN

Direct Seller

Business Name: My Happy Snappy Jewellery

Name: Linda Gienow

Address: P.O. Box 23 Craven, SK S0G 0W0

Phone: (306)731-3619

Email: gienow90@gmail.com

Website: www.mymagnoliaandvine.ca/C863

Social Media: My Happy Snappy Jewellery on Facebook.

Products Sold: Magnolia and Vine®.

CUDWORTH

Event Name: Hare Today, Gone Tomorrow Tradeshow

Date and Time: March 16, 2019, 10AM-4PM

Event Address: 605 1st Avenue

Website: https://www.4-paws-games-and-publishing.ca/haretodaygonetomorrow2019.html

Social Media: https://www.facebook.com/CudworthHareToday

Event Description: Come and enjoy some shopping at the first annual "Hare Today, Gone Tomorrow." Home-based business products, baking, crafts, books and more. A colouring table courtesy of Freckles the Bunny Series, items for kids to buy, paint and then take home. Kids tattoos, and free coffee. Come visit Poohka the rabbit between 11AM-2PM. The first 50 kids will get a treat (Poohka and the treat are free). Spots are $25 for an 8-foot table 2 8-foot tables/$40. We also have 11-foot tables for $35.

Free admission. Kitchen is being run a local group fundraising and the door prizes will support the Bruno Friendship Centre which occurred water damage this year. Should this change, we will announce the change on our Facebook page and announce another group to help.

Organizer Name: 4 Paws Games and Publishing; Vickianne Caswell

Organizer Phone: 639-994-7297 or 639-994-PAWS

Organizer Email: Admin@4-Paws-Games-and-Publishing.ca

Vendor Types Accepted: Mixed variety.

Event Name: For the Love of Her Event

Date and Time: May 4, 2019, 10AM-4PM

Event Address: 605 1st Avenue

Website: https://www.4-paws-games-and-publishing.ca/fortheloveofherevent2019.html

Social Media: www.facebook.com/CudworthFortheLoveofHerEvent

Event Description: The event is all about moms. Come out and do some shopping, learn some beauty techniques, or bring the kids out for some fun and a chance to make some nice Mother's Day gifts to take home. There will be some great door prizes, so don't forget to bring a non-perishable or monetary donation which goes to support the Cudworth Lion's Club Food Bank. There will also be special prizes (free entry) for mom's so make sure to come down!

Organizer Name: 4 Paws Games and Publishing; Vickianne Caswell

Organizer Phone: 639-994-7297 or 639-994-PAWS

Organizer Email: Admin@4-Paws-Games-and-Publishing.ca

Vendor Types Accepted: Mixed variety.

DELISLE

Handmade

Business Name: CE Signs

Name: Colton Edwards

Address: Box 806, Delisle, SK, S0L0P0

Phone: 306-220-2476

Email: cd.edwards@sasktel.net

Website: www.cncsigns.ca

Products Sold: Wood signs and plaques for acreages or cabins. Custom wood projects, like growth charts, cutting boards, dinosaurs etc.

HERBERT

Business Name: Love Apparel® by Kezia

Name: Kezia Menzies

Phone: 306-774-2192

Email: Kezijacks@hotmail.com

Products Sold: Clothing such as leggings, tops, dresses, and skirts. Willing to travel.

Direct Sellers

TUPPERWARE
All you need for the perfect meal

Patti Wacholtz
Consultant

Box 3236
Humboldt, Sask.
S0K2A0
(306)231-8121

patricia.wacholtz@gmail.com
pattiwacholtz@mytupperware.ca

Handmade

Fencepost Honey Farm

Patricia Wacholtz
Box 3236
Humboldt, Sask.
S0K 2A0

(306)231-8121

Patricia.Wacholtz@gmail.com

Nature at its best...pure sweet honey

Others

African Butterfly Hair Clips

Women Helping Women

(306)231-8121

Patricia Wacholtz   Patricia.Wacholtz@gmail.com

MARTENSVILLE

Artistic

Business Name: Sprinkles the Clown

Name: Deseri Adrian

Address: Box 43 Martensville, SK S0K 2T0

Phone: 780-872-1288

Email: sprinklesclown@yahoo.ca

Website: http://sprinklestheclown.webs.com

MELFORT

Business Name: Pillow Talk

Name: Wendy Hurd

Address: Box 3012 Melfort, SK S0E 1A0

Phone: 306-921-9897

Email: pillowtalkwhl@gmail.com

Social Media: https://www.facebook.com/pillowtalkwlh

Products Sold: Unique homemade pillowscapes to add a dramatic, decorative accent to any home, cabin, or workspace.

MIDDLE LAKE

Business Name: Sunday Drive

Name: Andrea Carroll

Phone: 306-231-9205

Email: andrea@sundaydrive.ca

Website: www.sundaydrive.ca

Social Media: https://www.facebook.com/sundaydrive.ca

Services: Maps and advertising that uncover niche markets and promote shop local initiatives.

MOOSE JAW

Business Name: Magnolia and Vine®

Name: Denise Konieczny

Phone: (306) 631-7893

Email: mav.denise@shaw.ca

Website: www.mymagnoliaandvine.ca/c451

Social Media: www.facebook.com/snapstylebydenise

Products Sold: Snap-style customizable jewellery and interchangeable fashion accessories.

Business Name: TeaLife®

Name: Joanne Marta

Phone: (306) 313-8769

Email: joannestealife@gmail.com

Website: www.tealife.ca/biz/jmarta

Social Media: Facebook @Joannestealife

Products Sold: Quality loose leaf teas and accessories.

Business Name: Norwex®

Name: Edith Scholz

Phone: (306) 267-4400

Email: e.scholz@sasktel.net

Website: www.edithscholz.norwex.biz

Products Sold: Cleaning supplies without chemicals. Products for use in your home and in personal care.

Handmade

Business Name: Surrayah'sJewels

Name: Elaine Gill

Phone: 306-693-4193

Email: e.gill@sasktel.net

Social Media: https://www.facebook.com/SurrayahsJewels

Products Sold: Hand-crafted jewellery and accessories specializing in seed bead weaving/bead embroidery, wire wrapping and hand painted pendants.

Business Name: Woodrose and Sapphire Jewelry

Name: Richelle Leptich

Phone: 306-630-4946

Email: mamasvenue@gmail.com

Website: www.mamasvenue.com

Social Media: https://www.facebook.com/groups/woodrose

Products Sold: Bracelets, earrings, necklaces, rings, wine markers, bookmarks with interchangeable gems that let you match your own style, body jewellery, nose rings and navel rings.

Direct Sellers

Business Name: Thrive Life Foods

Name: Brenda Georget

Phone: (306) 940-8910

Email: thrivewithBrenda@mail.com

Website: https://canada.thrivelife.com/thrivewithbrenda

Social Media: https://www.facebook.com/Thrive-Goodies-320569078558073

Products Sold: Freeze dried food makes meal preparations faster, simpler, and more convenient without neglecting taste and quality.

THRIVE LIFE
Simple. Clean. Food.

Brenda Georget
Independent Consultant

Phone: (306) 940-8910

Email: thrivewithbrenda@mail.com
www.thrivewithbrenda.thrivelife.com

RABBIT LAKE

Direct Seller

Business Name: Puretrim® (Mediterranean Wellness)

Name: Doreen Lamb

Address: Box 37 Rabbit Lake, SK S0M 2L0

Phone: (306) 824-4450

Email: ddlamb@sasktel.net

Website: www.dlamb.puretrim.com

Social Media: N/A

Products Sold: Meal replacements, Boost tea®, Daily Complete vit's Experience®, Liver Master®, and Synergy Defense®. Puretrim Joint tea®, Pure Garden Skin Serum®, Joint Health Starter Pac®, 30-day weight loss challenge, 10-day weight loss challenge, and 30-day Liver master cleanse.

REGINA

Business Name: Elevacity

Name: Tina Woronoski

Address: Regina, SK

Phone: 306-539-3371

Email: elevate.tina@gmail.com

Website: https://elevacity.com/tinaleanne

Social Media: https://www.facebook.com/groups/1921354694782852

Products Sold: Happy Coffee and Xanthama.

Business Name: Terra Firma®

Name: Frank Boehm

Phone: (306) 530-3962

Email: frank.boehm@sasktel.net

Products Sold: Stone and crystal jewelry as well as diffuser bracelets.

Business Name: PRUVIT®

Name: Tess Boehm

Phone: (306) 529-2850

Email: pruvit@sasktel.net

Website: www.tessboehm.ShopKeto.com

Social Media: www.facebook.com/reginapruvit

Products Sold: Exogenous Ketones®, Keto Kreme® for Bulletproof Coffee®, and MCT oil.

Business Name: Elevacity®

Name: Frank Boehm

Phone: (306) 530-3962

Email: elevacity@sasktel.net

Website: www.elevacity.com/frankboehm

Social Media: www.facebook.com/elepreneurscanada

Products Sold: Smart Coffee®, Hot Chocolate, Keto Creamer®, "Happy Pills®," vitamin patches and weight loss coffee.

Business Name: VoxxLife

Name: Chantelle Ayers

Phone: 306-550-4612

Email: chanie.ayers@gmail.com

Website: https://111125652.voxxlife.com

Social Media: https://www.facebook.com/Voxx-Your-Life-with-Chantelle-240246636681828

Products Sold: HPT socks, insoles, patches...much more coming out.

Business Name: Young Living®

Name: Tess Boehm

Phone: (306) 529-2850

Email: younglivingregina@sasktel.net

Website: www.youngliving.org/tessboehm

Social Media: www.facebook.com/younglivingregina

Products Sold: Oils, roller balls, healing crystals and more.

Handmade

Business Name: Kids N Kats – Sewing Creations

Name: Christine Euteneier

Email: kidsnkats@sasktel.net

Website: www.kidsnkats@sasktel.net

Social Media: www.facebook.com/kidsnkatssewingcreations

Products Sold: Specializing in yoga props. Bolsters covered foam blocks, yoga straps, meditation cushions and sets, eye pillows, and yoga mat bags. A line of pillows and bags are available and custom orders for those unique products that can't be found on the market, are always welcome.

ROSE VALLEY

Business Name: TLC Tanya's Leggings Clothing and Accessories

Name: Tanya Boey

Address: Box 491 Rose Valley, SK S0E 1M0

Phone: 306-370-4433

Email: tanyaboey@yahoo.ca

Social Media: https://www.facebook.com/groups/1581742522091590

Products Sold: Leggings, tops, skirts, jeggings, and C.C. Beanies.

ROSTHERN

Business Name: Fire Moon Soap Company

Name: Louisa Reddekopp

Address: Box 52 Rosthern, SK S0K 3R0

Phone: 306-349-9420

Email: firemoonsoap@gmail.com

Social Media: https://www.facebook.com/firemoonsoapco

Products Sold: Handmade soaps, rose petal salve, lip balm, beard oil, Aloe Vera spray, smudge sprays, room & linen sprays. All made with natural, locally sourced, organic ingredients whenever possible.

SASKATOON

Business Name: Seacret Direct

Name: Bonnie Clemence

Phone: 306-280-4917

Email: b.clemence@hotmail.com

Website: www.seacretdirect.com/bclemence

Social Media: https://www.facebook.com/seacretskinforthewin

Products Sold: Dead Sea mineral skincare, haircare, bodycare, as well as well as nutrition.

Business Name: J.R. Watkins by Lynnette Bates

Name: Lynnette Bates

Phone: 306-203-1364

Email: lynnette@sasktel.net

Website: https://www.respectedhomebusiness.com/793223

Social Media: https://www.facebook.com/Watkins-by-Lynnette-Bates-922303274573432

Products Sold: Homecare products such as cleaners, laundry soap, and mosquito spray. Body care products such as washes, soaps, and lotions. Remedies such as medicated ointment, bath soaks and Petro Carbo.

Business Name: Stephanie's Totes and Home

Name: Stephanie Kelsey

Phone: (306) 270-8308

Email: stephanie-kelsey@hotmail.com

Website: www.mythirtyone.ca/skelsey

Social Media: Stephanie's Totes and Home Facebook group.

Products Sold: 31 Gifts®. Home storage and organization; travel accessories and luggage; purses; totes; wallets; home décor. Most products can be customized with names or icons.

Handmade
Business Name: Lalita

Name: Gladys Prentice

Phone: (306) 220-3831

Email: gfprentice59@gmail.com

Social Media: On Facebook.

Products Sold: Wedding and children's accessories.

Business Name: Handmade by LyLi

Name: Lynn Dufort and Linton Davenport

Phone: (306) 717-9094

Email: le.dufort@sasktel.net

Website: N/A

Social Media: Handmade by LyLi on Facebook.

Products Sold: Doll bunkbed/single bed with mattress and bedding. Doll receiving blankets, doll cradle with mattress, doll high chairs, children's car organizers, snap bags, colour again pillows, and children's shelf for Matchbox® cars or knickknacks. Microwave bowls, hair towels, thread and bobbin racks, ironing board extension cord holders, and Saskatchewan Roughrider coolers.

Business Name: Prairie Princess Bowtique

Email: prairieprincessbows@gmail.com

Social Media: www.facebook.com/prairieprincessbowtique

Products Sold: Hair accessories such as headbands and hair clips made with a variety of materials. Newborn to adult sizes. Offering ready made items and custom orders.

Others

Business Name: Rosette Events

Name: Michelle Whalen

Phone: 306-717-4297

Email: rosette.events.mw@gmail.com

Social Media: https://www.facebook.com/rosette.events

Services: Creative and elegant event design and planning. Rosette Events organizes tradeshows, markets and other family-oriented events, and the profits are donated to charities in the community. Take the stress away from planning your next social event with our affordable and stress-free planning services for any event. Servicing Saskatoon and area.

Business Name: L & L Business Services

Name: Lynn Dufort and Linton Davenport

Phone: (306) 717-9094

Email: le.dufort@sasktel.net

Website: N/A

Social Media: N/A

Products Sold: T1 Personal Tax services and T2 Corporate Tax services.

Event Name: Zenith

Date and Time: August 4th, 10am-4pm

Event Address: German Cultural Centre, 160 Cartwright St E

Social Media: https://www.facebook.com/rosette.events

Event Description: A summer faire and market with proceeds donated to charity.

Organizer Name: Rosette Events, Michelle Whalen

Organizer Phone: 306-717-4297

Organizer Email: rosette.events.mw@gmail.com

Vendor Types Accepted: Mixed variety.

Event Name: Harvest Home

Date and Time: October 6th, 10am-4pm

Event Address: German Cultural Centre, 160 Cartwright St E

Social Media: https://www.facebook.com/rosette.events

Event Description: A medieval Halloween market and family fun event with proceeds donated to the Ronald McDonald House Charities Saskatchewan.

Organizer Name: Rosette Events, Michelle Whalen

Organizer Phone: 306-717-4297

Organizer Email: rosette.events.mw@gmail.com

Vendor Types Accepted: Mixed variety.

Event Name: Sugar Plums

Date and Time: Nov 9th 10am-4pm

Event Address: German Cultural Centre, 160 Cartwright St E

Social Media: https://www.facebook.com/rosette.events

Organizer Name: Rosette Events, Michelle Whalen

Organizer Phone: 306-717-4297

Organizer Email: rosette.events.mw@gmail.com

Vendor Types Accepted: Mixed variety.

Event Name: Yuletide Shimmer

Date and Time: December 1st, 10am-4pm

Event Address: German Cultural Centre, 160 Cartwright St E

Social Media: https://www.facebook.com/rosette.events

Event Description: A royal winter wonderland and market with proceeds donated to the Saskatoon Crisis Nursery.

Organizer Name: Rosette Events, Michelle Whalen

Organizer Phone: 306-717-4297

Organizer Email: rosette.events.mw@gmail.com

Vendor Types Accepted: Mixed variety.

WEYBURN

Direct Seller

Business Name: Elavacity®

Name: Stephanie Loreth

Phone: (306) 891-4651

Email: weger_1@hotmail.com

Website: www.elevacity.com/StephanieLoreth

Social Media: Steph's New Adventures and Energized Way of Living Life page on Facebook.

Products Sold: Smart Coffee®: Columbian instant coffee which supports efforts to control appetite and enhance mental focus.

Xanthamax®: Supports well-being; Choclevate®: Delicious hot chocolate that supports efforts to control appetite and enhance mental focus; KetoCre®: Effective, delicious, and nutritious ketogenic creamer; Vitamin Patches®: Nutraceutical-based health in a patch. Energy, sleep, and hangover patches; Pure®: Removes heavy metals and toxins from body; Timeless®: Skincare for men and women; Elier Mud®: purifies and infuses skin with vital nutrients; and Elier Serum®: Control time and care for skin.

YOUNG

Business Name: Tender Paws Pet Products

Name: Tanya Nagy

Address: Box 43 Young, SK S0K 4Y0

Phone: 306-380-3653

Email: tenderpawspetproducts@gmail.com

Website: www.tenderpawspetproducts.weebly.com

Social Media: https://www.facebook.com/TenderPawsPetBalm

Products Sold: Homemade and organic pet balms, toys, and treats. Our products are a safe solution for all your training needs, including outdoor protection in hot or cold weather. Proudly Canadian made in a small prairie town.

www.ingramcontent.com/pod-product-compliance
Lightning Source LLC
Chambersburg PA
CBHW051427200326

41520CB00023B/7389